Cave Creatures
of
Glenwood Caverns

by

David B. Steinmann
Research Associate
Denver Museum of Nature & Science

Publisher:
Professional Wetlands Consulting, Inc.
Boulder, Colorado 80302

ISBN-13: 978-1-48-021647-1
ISBN-10: 1-4802-1647-X

Front Cover: A male pseudoscorpion of a new species named *Cryptocreagris steinmanni*, an ancient and predatory arachnid that eats other cave life. They are small and harmless to humans, and can be found living throughout the cave. Denver Museum of Nature & Science catalog # ZA.23949.

A reflective pool of water within Glenwood Caverns is habitat for cave species.

I would like to thank Steve and Jeanne Beckley and Phil Kriz for allowing me to collect cave invertebrates from Glenwood Caverns and to explore the cave. Thank you to Micah Ball who first saw the new species of pseudoscorpion and who showed me where to find them. I would also like to thank all of the cavers and people who assisted me in finding, collecting and identifying the new species of cave life at Glenwood Caverns, especially my wife Debbie Steinmann and our bug-finding son Nathaniel.

Thank you to the Zoology Department at the Denver Museum of Nature & Science, the Lloyd David and Carlye Cannon Wattis Foundation, the Zocchi Foundation, and the National Speleological Society for providing funding to facilitate my cave research. Photographs were taken at the University of Colorado, Entomology Department with help from Virginia Scott and Andrew Hicks, and scanning electron microscope pictures were taken at the University of Colorado Geology Department by Dr. Fred Luiszer.

Introduction

Glenwood Caverns in Glenwood Springs, Colorado is an underground oasis with over two dozen species that are visible to the naked eye living in the cave. While walking through the cave one is first attracted to the spectacular speleothems, while looking closer allows us to see that the cave is full of tiny forms of life. There are at least 8 new and previously unknown species in the cave, most of which are rare and only known to live within Glenwood Caverns. The cave has spiders, pseudoscorpions, springtails, millipedes, centipedes, crickets, flies, mites, beetles, bats and harvestmen. This book shows some of the actual species found living in the cave as photographed under a microscope.

Many of the species are albino with well-developed sensory organs, and are totally adapted to live in the dark and cool cave environment. Cave-adapted creatures are often small and without eyes, and they can have elongated legs and are long-lived. The invertebrates living in Glenwood Caverns are predators, omnivores and scavengers. They can eat organic matter, bacteria, scat and fungus, while predators eat other cave creatures.

There are four types of cave inhabitants:
1) Troglobites are obligate cave dwellers and are restricted to caves.
2) Troglophiles live and reproduce in caves but are not restricted to caves.
3) Trogloxenes utilize caves, but leave caves for feeding or other purposes.
4) Accidentals enter or wander into caves, which are not their usual habitat.

Dave Steinmann collects cave life with tweezers. Photo by Norm Thompson.

Springtail (Collembola), an eyeless and albino troglobite in the genus *Tomocerus*. Seven different species of springtail live in Glenwood Caverns. They are omnivores and scavengers, found near old wood, small pools of water, and organic matter. The forked tail, or furcula, is folded beneath the body and can be rapidly extended to spring the individual far into the air, helping them escape from predators. Collembola are classified as arthropods, and are similar to insects. Springtails are some of the oldest arthropod lineages in the world, as fossil springtails that are over 400 million years old have been found. Many springtails can survive without food for a very long time. Nearly every Colorado cave has springtails. The one in this photo is a likely new species, it was found deep within the cave near a pool of water.

Albino springtail in the genus *Entomobrya* that is covered with fine hairs that aid in navigating the underground environment in total darkness. It is a troglobite closely related to springtails presently only known from South Dakota caves. This springtail was found near Exclamation Point in the year 2000.

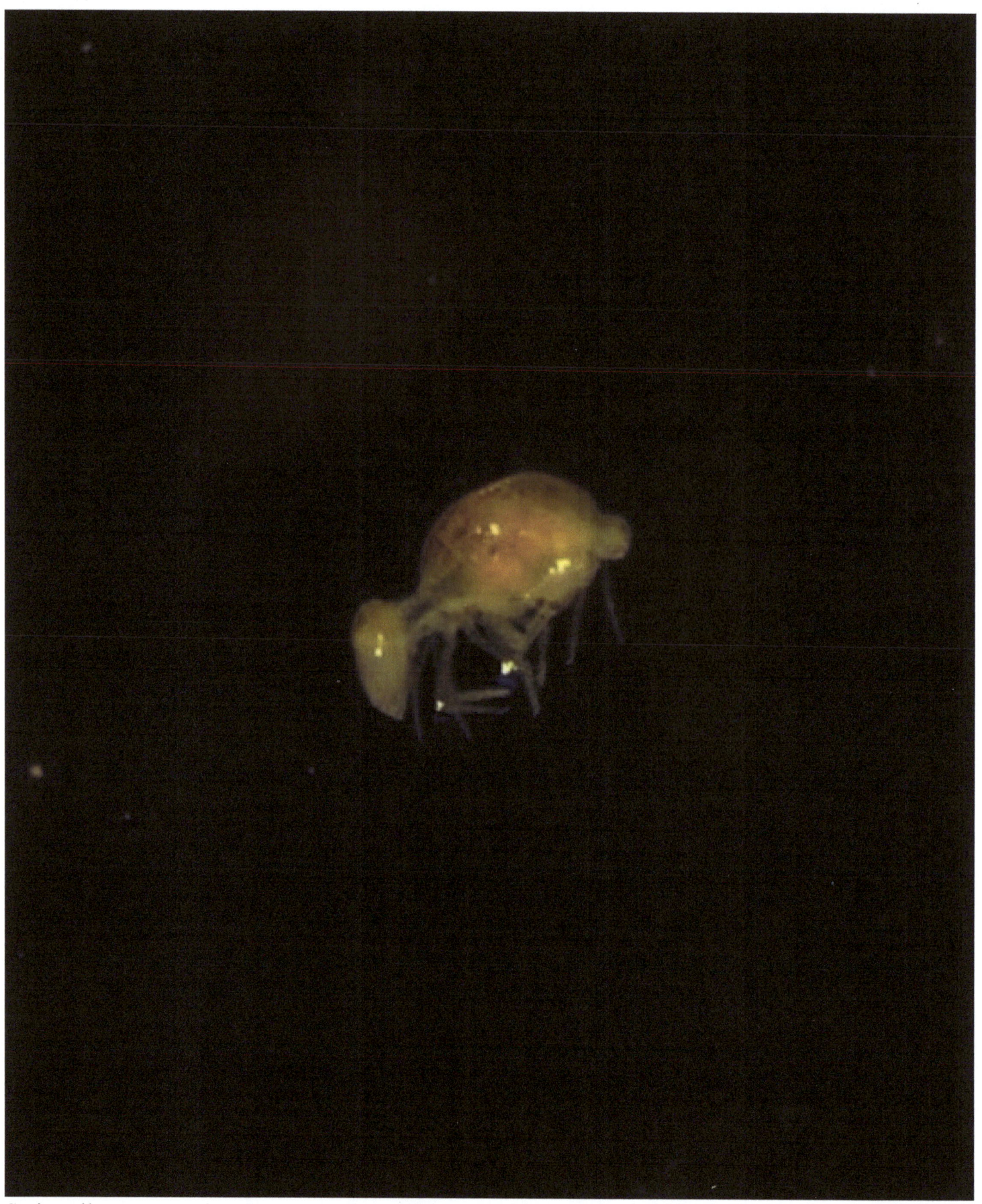

Springtail, a new species that was named *Arrhopalites hubbardi,* a tiny and eyeless troglobite adapted to the Glenwood Caverns environment. Many of the little pools and small puddles of water within the cave have these springtails living on the water surface, they are the size of a speck of dust and hard to see.

A scanning electron micrograph showing overlapping scales on the body of a springtail, magnified 1,250 times after the springtail was coated with a thin layer of gold. Photograph by Dr. Fred Luiszer.

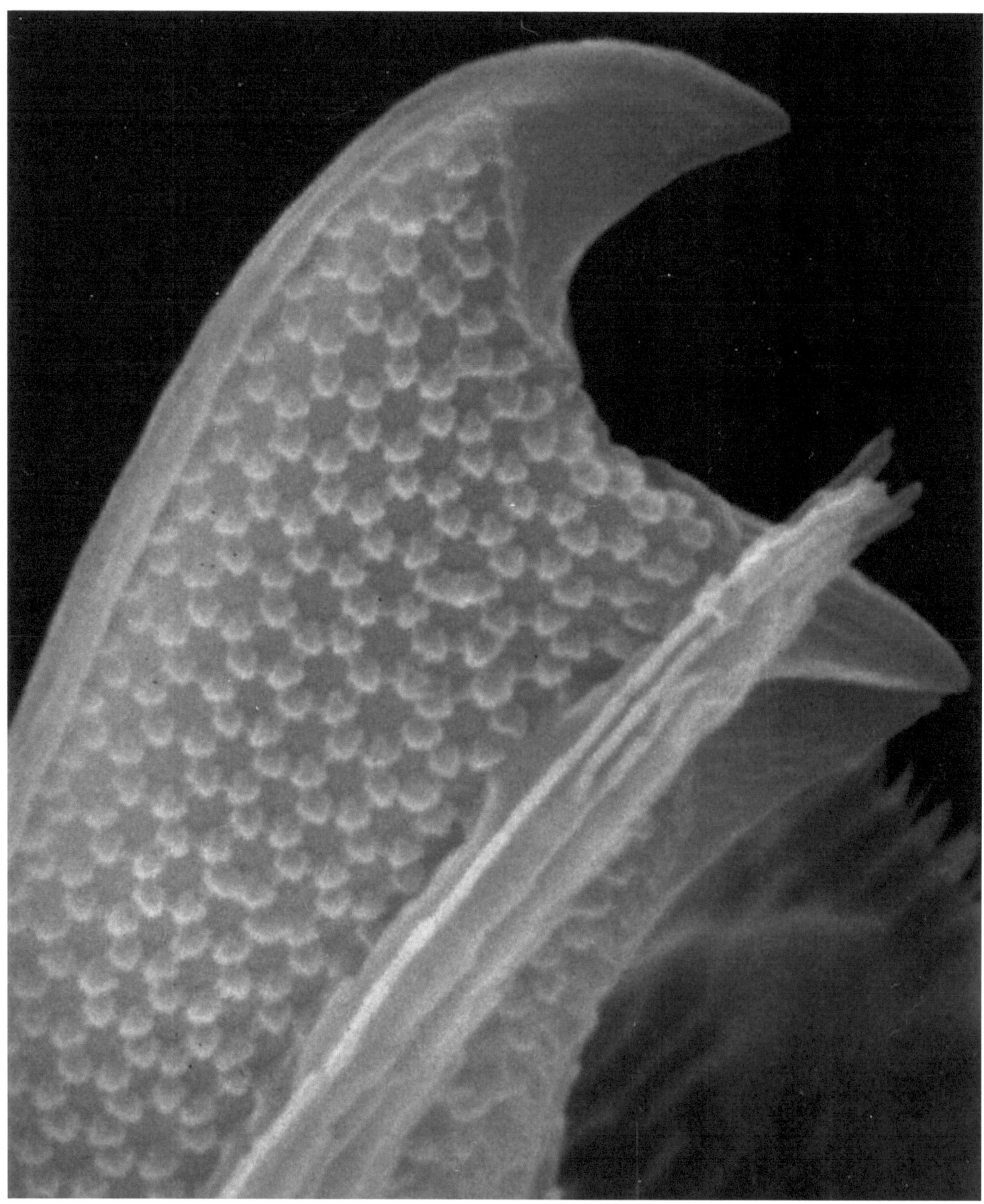

Repeating hexagonal patterns on the forked tail appendage (furcula) of a springtail, magnified 10,000 times under a scanning electron microscope. Photograph by Dr. Fred Luiszer.

A close-up picture of the symmetrical and repeating patterns on the body of a springtail, magnified over 10,000 times under a scanning electron microscope. Photograph by Dr. Fred Luiszer.

Dipluran, a new species in the genus Haplocampa which is albino, eyeless and harmless. They eat organic matter, like fungi and bacteria. These diplurans have tail appendages called cerci which detach and wiggle when the dipluran is being chased, similar to a lizard losing its tail to distract the predator.

Spider, a troglophile named *Arcuphantes cavaticus* that likes to live in caves. It builds small webs in crevices and cracks that are used to entangle and catch food. Eight eyes are present along with numerous sensory hairs on the body and legs. Denver Museum of Nature & Science catalog # ZA.4862.

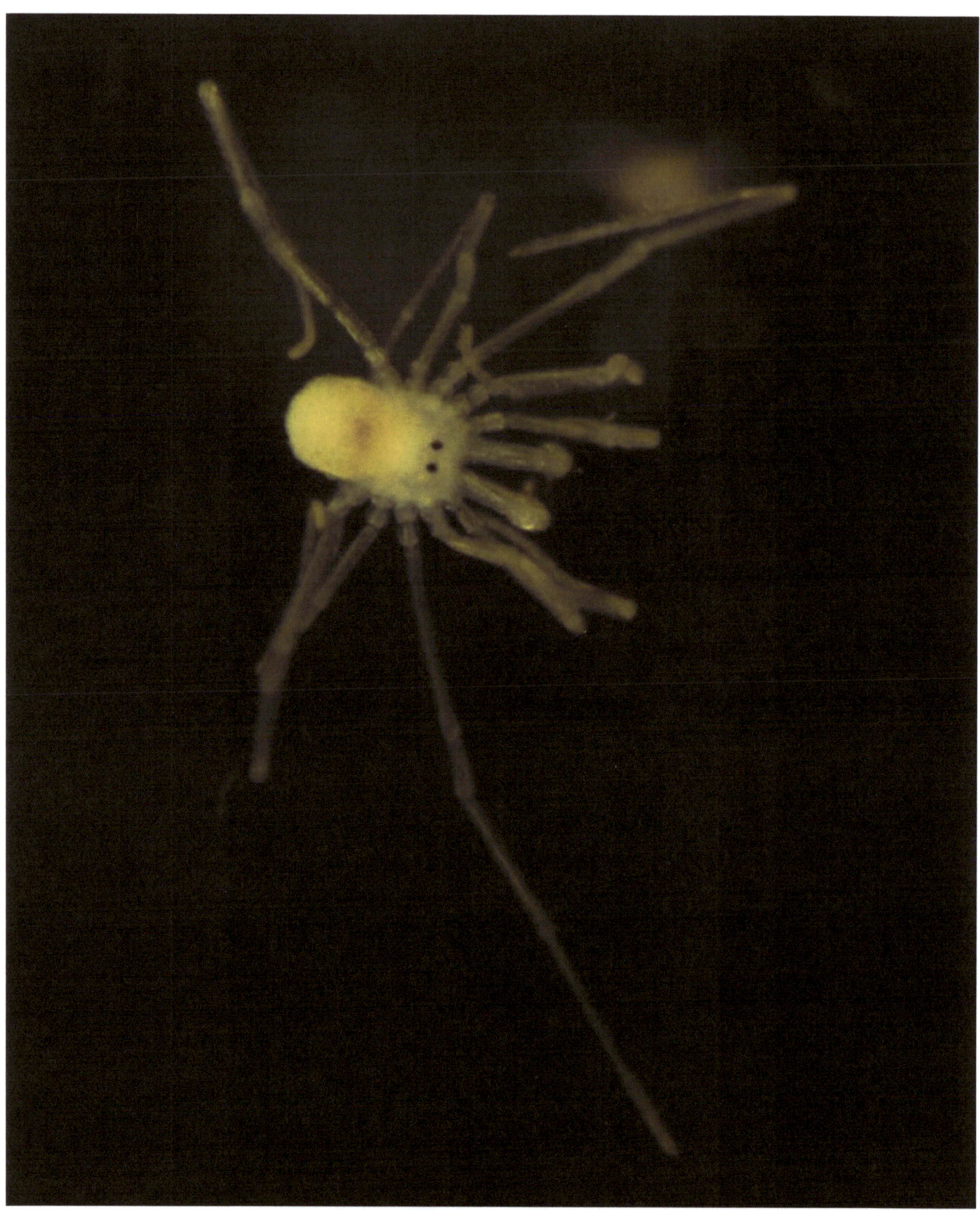

Harvestmen, a daddy longlegs in the order Opiliones. This specimen is immature with a pale color and elongated legs. The adults are larger and darker in color. They feed on organic material, prey on smaller cave life, and are most often found close to the cave entrances. This species is in the genus *Taracus*.

The claw-like mouthparts called chelicera on the cave harvestmen on page 10, used to catch and devour prey such as springtails, mites and insects. Magnified 180 times. Photograph taken by Dr. Fred Luiszer.

Fly, an undetermined species in the order Diptera that lives in Glenwood Caverns. They navigate in the total darkness of Glenwood Caverns, and sometimes become food for cave spiders and other underground predators. This species probably detects airflow and other cues to find their way.

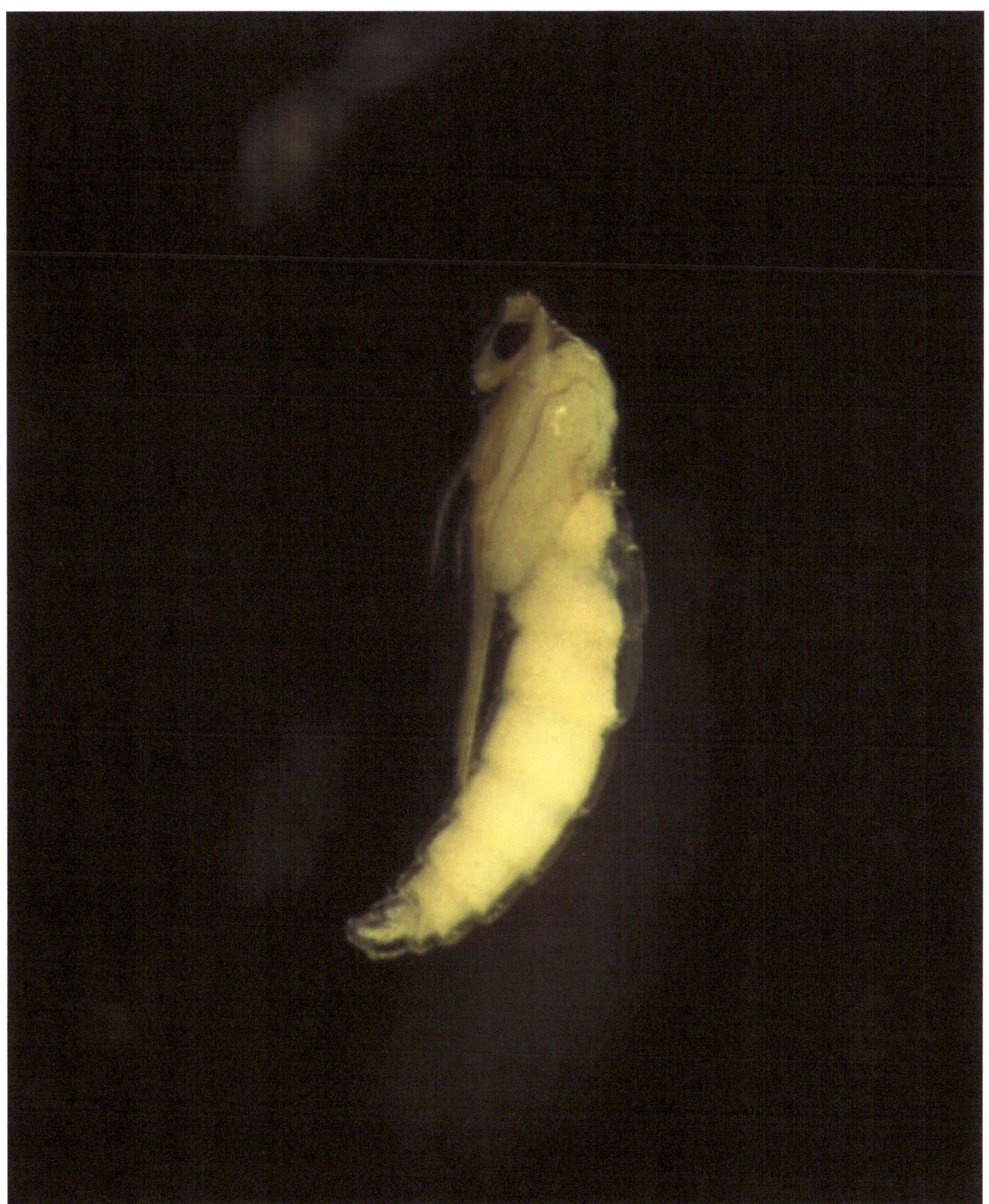

Pupa of the fly shown on the previous page, found under a small stone in a moist section of the cave near organic matter. This pupa has begun to develop compound eyes, wings and antennae. They need to have consistently high humidity and damp earth to emerge successfully as adults after hatching from tiny eggs.

Rove beetle named *Quedius spelaeus* that is a common cave inhabitant in Colorado, a troglophile that is an omnivorous scavenger. Rove beetles can be seen under rocks where the soils are damp. This innocuous species has eyes, is pigmented and is most numerous in the twilight zone near cave entrances.

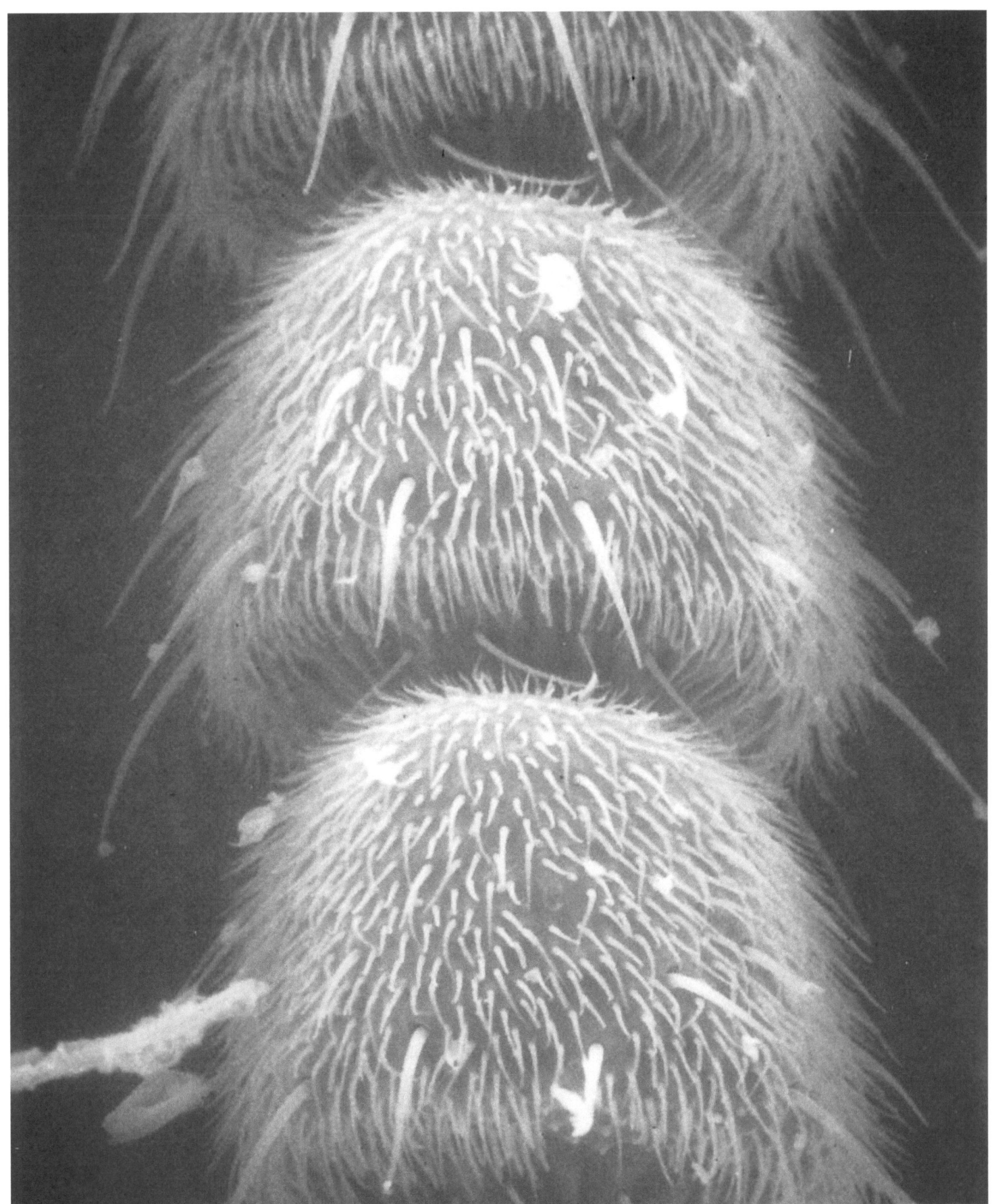

Rove beetle antenna, magnified 264 times under a scanning electron microscope, with hundreds of tactile hairs on each segment that help the beetles sense their environment and find food. This photo is a close-up from the beetle specimen shown on the previous page. Photograph by Dr. Fred Luiszer.

Rove beetle leg from the specimen shown on page 14, illustrating the pointed spikes and sharp hairs located near a leg joint, magnified 142 times under a scanning electron microscope. These structures help the beetles move and burrow through soft cave soils. Photograph by Dr. Fred Luiszer.

Flea found in an old packrat nest before Glenwood Caverns was open to the public. Dr. Helen Pigage with the U.S. Air Force Academy in Colorado Springs determined it to be *Amaradix bitterootensis*. They are an accidental and uncommon cave inhabitant. Denver Museum of Nature & Science catalog # ZE.2933.

Millipede, *Austrotyla coloradensis*, a troglophile that is nearly albino with some tan pigmentation. This millipede has eyes. It lives under rocks and near organic debris in moist parts of the cave. Millipedes have two pairs of legs per body segment, this species is an omnivore that is also present in other Colorado caves.

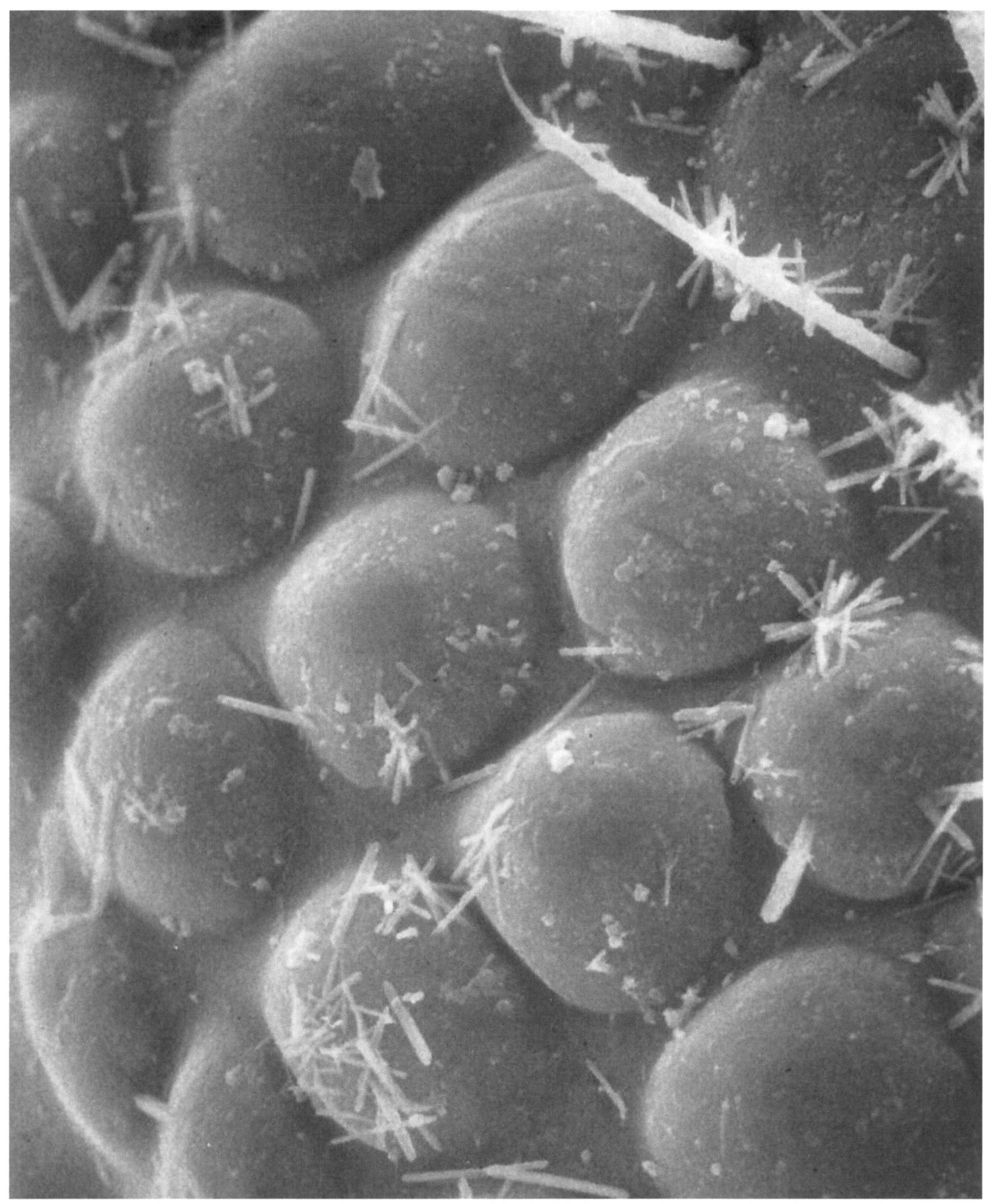

Eyes of the millipede *Austrotyla coloradensis* magnified 540 times under a scanning electron microscope, showing the symmetry of the compound eyes, and small hairs. Photograph by Dr. Fred Luiszer.

Centipede, a likely a new species in the order Lithobiomorpha. It is a troglophile with eyes and pigment. The fanged mouthparts of this fast moving arthropod contain venom, making centipede bites painful. Centipedes have one pair of legs per body segment, and are predators of smaller invertebrates.

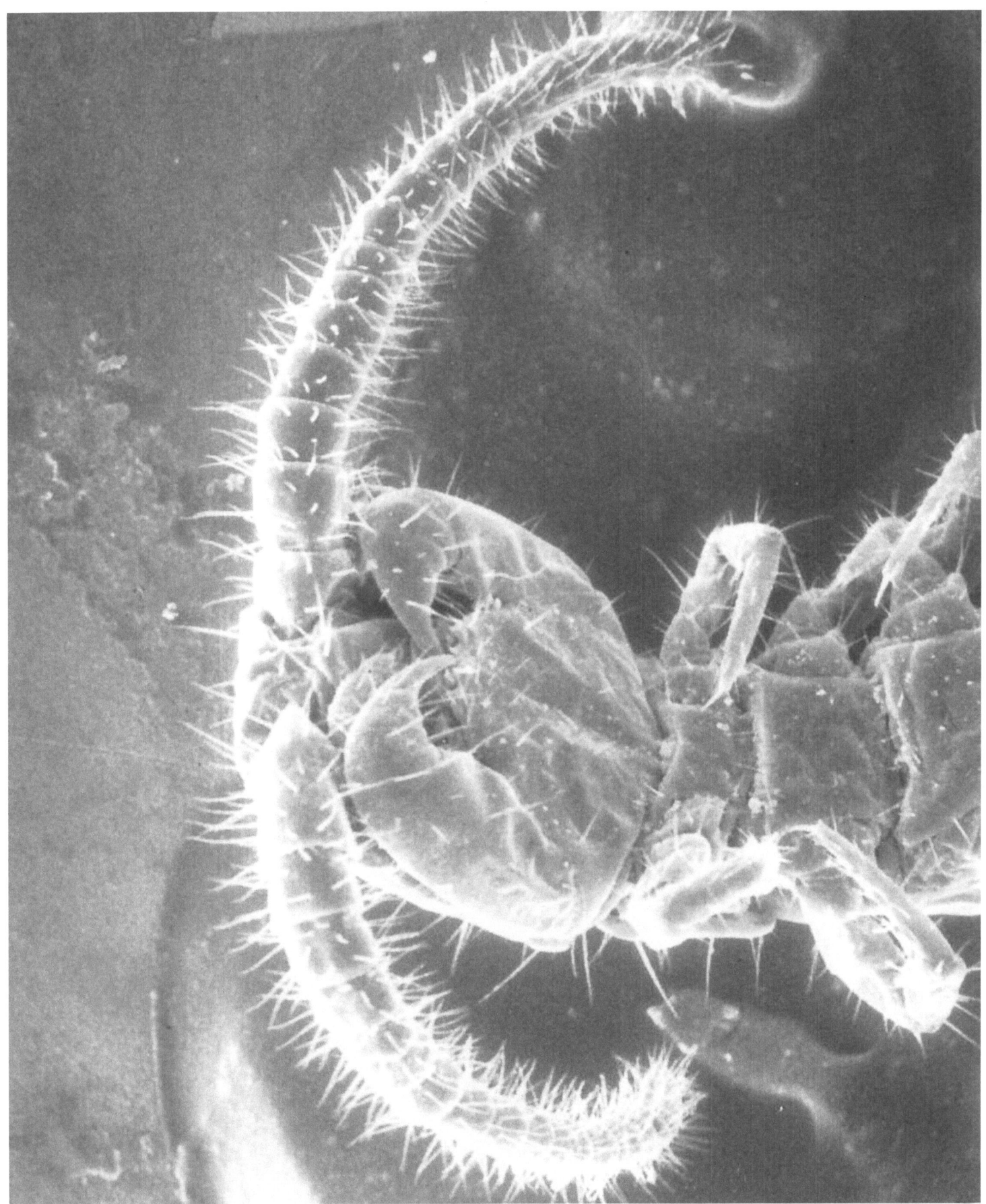

Centipede mouthparts and antennae showing the numerous small hairs and venomous mouthparts, taken under a scanning electron microscope. Magnified 43 times. Photograph by Dr. Fred Luiszer.

Springtail, a tiny new species named *Onychiurus steinmanni* that was discovered by the author. They live in both Glenwood Caverns and in Hubbard's Cave, which are on opposite sides of the Colorado River. This eyeless and albino species lives on pools of water and in the soil. Photo by Andrew Hicks.

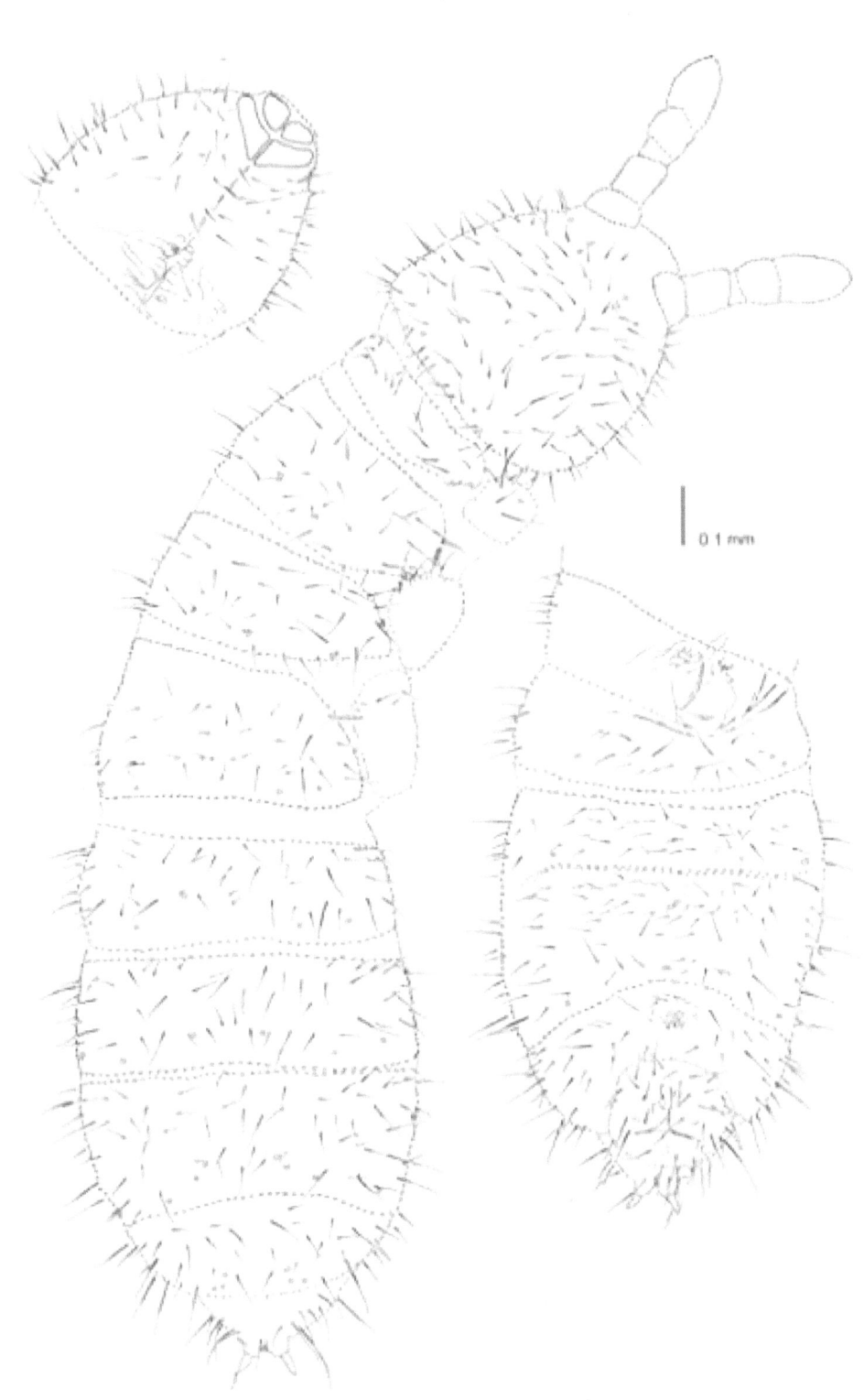

Illustration of *Onychiurus steinmanni* by Dr. Jacek Pomorski, used in the naming of this new species. The body is covered with fine hairs called setae that help these eyeless springtails survive underground in complete darkness where feel, smell and chemical receptors are used to move about and find food.

A female of a new pseudoscorpion species currently known only from Glenwood Caverns, named *Cryptogreagris steinmanni* after the author. It is a predator at the top of the cave food-chain. The long, claw-like appendages help capture prey. Denver Museum of Nature & Science catalog # ZA.23950.

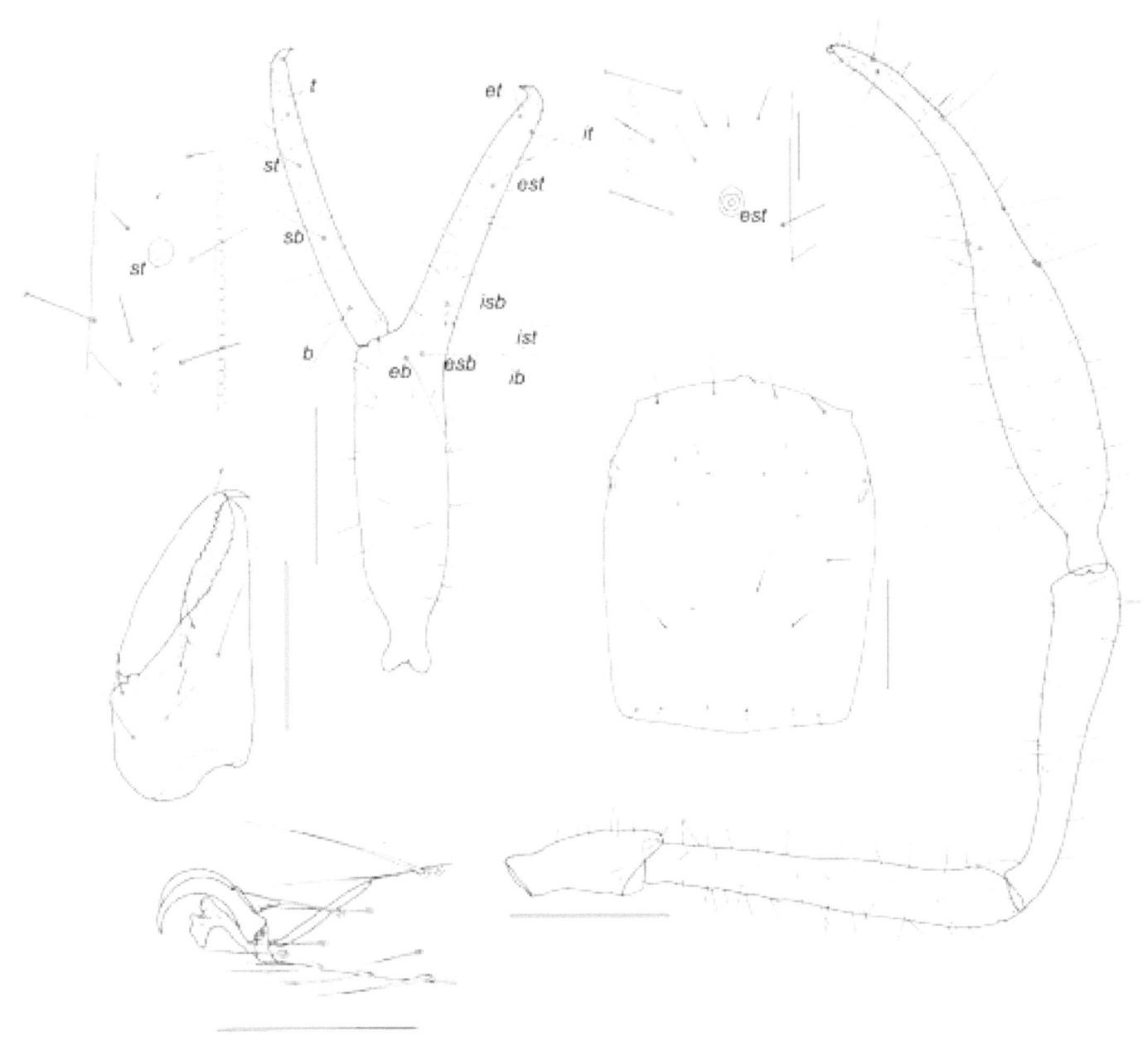

Illustration for the pseudoscorpion *Cryptocreagris steinmanni,* by Dr. Mark Harvey with the Western Australian Museum. The drawing shows some of the specific morphological details unique to this cave pseudoscorpion that were used to distinguish this new species from other known pseudoscorpions.

A cave cricket with elongated legs and very long antennae that are helpful when living in the dark. Cave crickets are agile and are capable of jumping high into the air. They like to congregate on cave walls and ceilings. As omnivores and scavengers, they may leave the cave to feed and drink while outside.

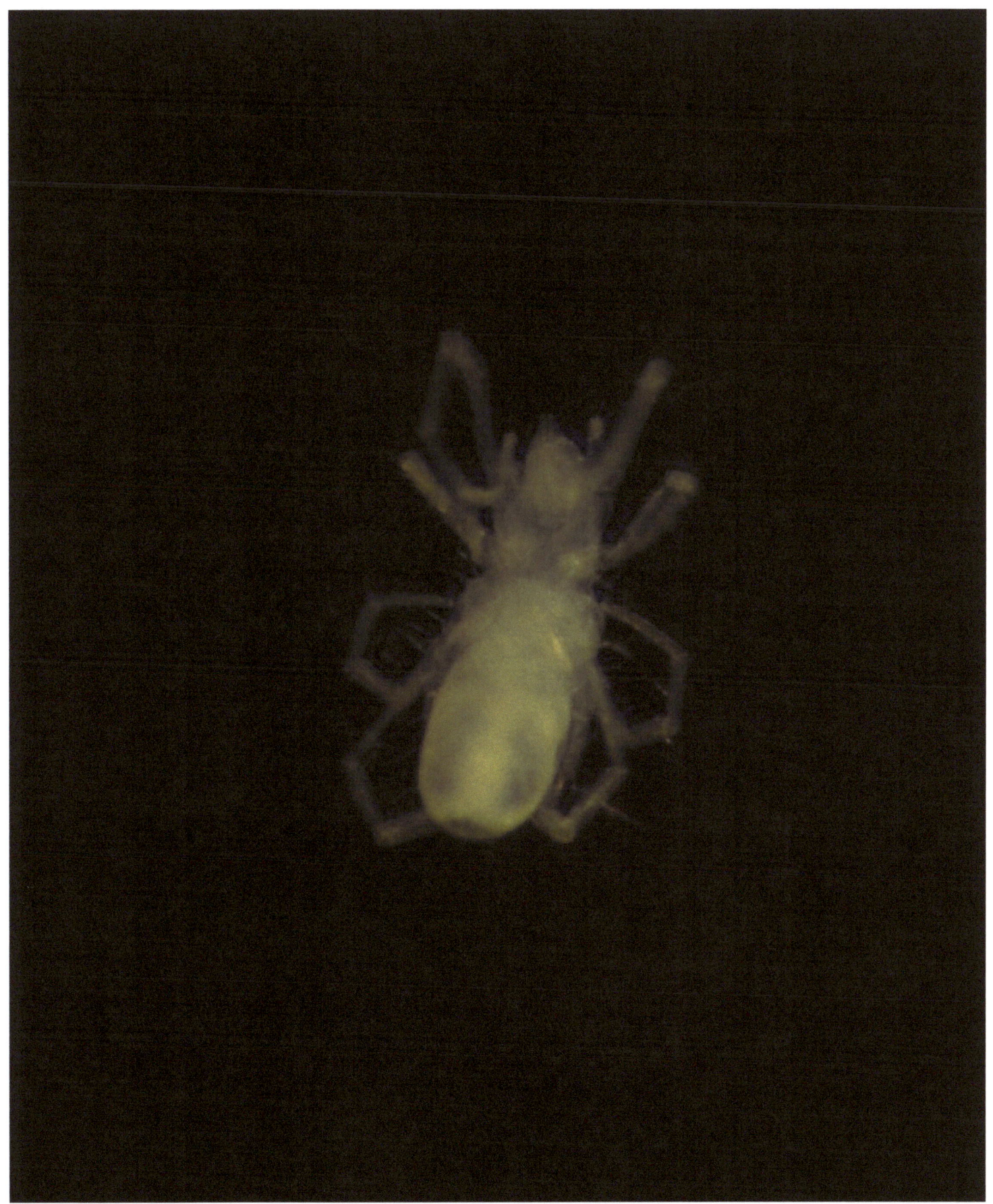

Mite, an undetermined and likely new species in the order Acari. This tiny and hairy mite can be found living under rocks and near old pieces of wood in the cave. It is both eyeless and albino with long sensory hairs all over its legs and body. They burrow into the soil, and are either troglobites or troglophiles.

A beetle in the family Leiodidae, a new species that has wings and can fly. They are small with two eyes, and are found in moist environments near cave entrances. This species has segmented antennae with the segments getting larger towards the tip. Only a few of these beetles have been found in the cave.

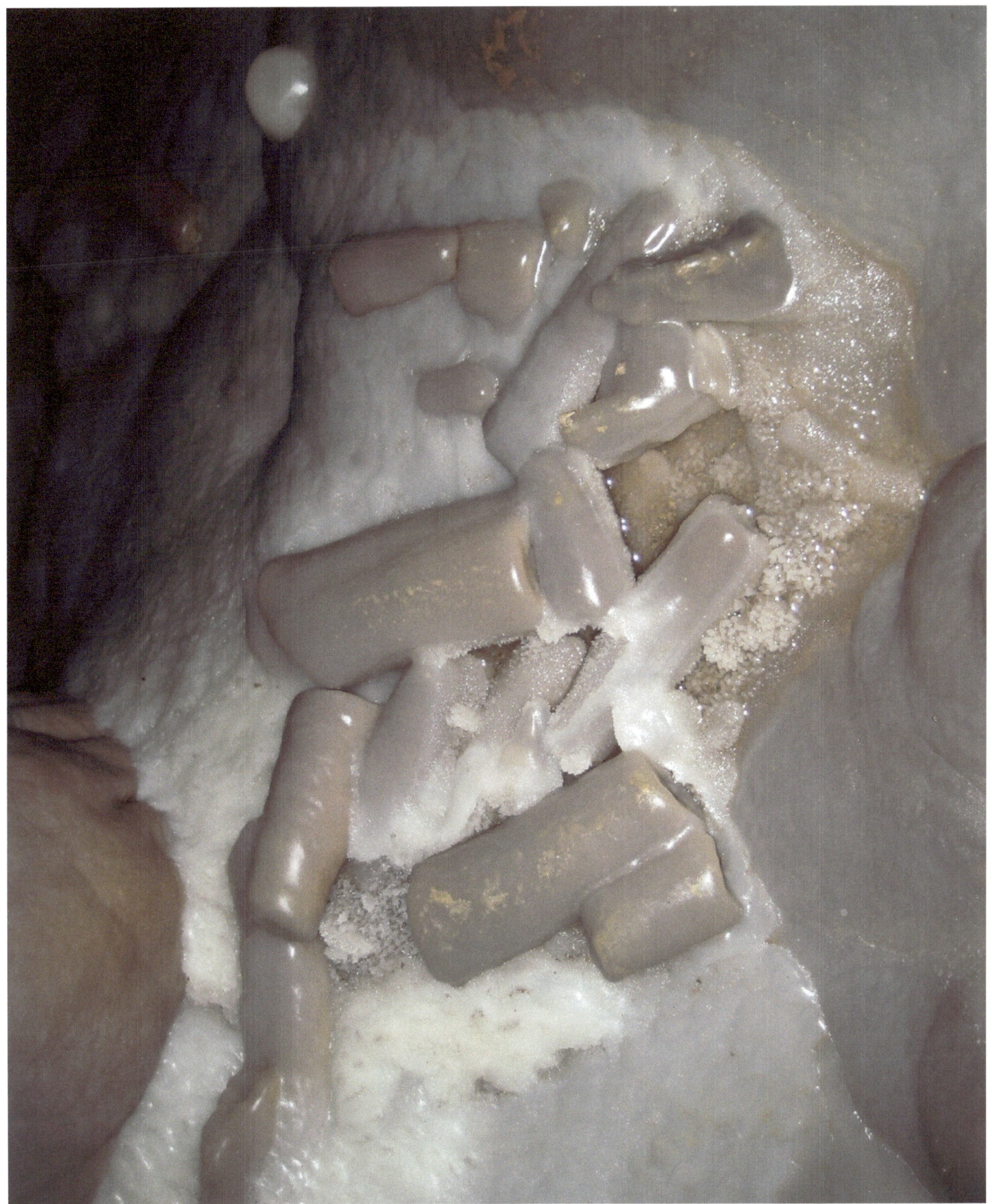

Broken stalactites and small pools of water in the Paradise section of Glenwood Caverns. These broken formations create wet and moist living spaces for several different cave species including springtails, diplurans, mites, millipedes, centipedes and pseudoscorpions.

A little brown bat hanging in a protected crevice in the wall, these mammals are native to Colorado. Bats hibernate in caves in the winter, and take shelter in caves during the day in warmer months. Colorado has 17 different bat species. They are an important part of the ecosystem as pollinators and insect eaters.

David Steinmann squirms his way out of a passage near Lame Haven in Glenwood Caverns.

Debbie, Dave & Nathan Steinmann enjoy the Alpine Coaster at Glenwood Caverns Adventure Park.

About the Author

David Steinmann is a biospeleologist, or cave biologist, who studies cave life in search of new species. David has a degree in Physics and Biology from the University of Colorado, and is a Research Associate with the Denver Museum of Nature & Science. He works as a wetlands biologist, and is a volunteer firefighter in Boulder County. David studies caves throughout Colorado, which has the highest elevation and coldest caves in the continental United States. His cave research requires climbing, crawling, squeezing and rappelling into total darkness, where he looks for cave-adapted life forms that are often eyeless and albino. So far, David discovered over 100 new species and several new genera in the caves of Colorado.

Three of the new species David discovered are named after him: the pseudoscorpion *Cryptogreagris steinmanni* from Glenwood Caverns, the springtail *Typhlogastrura steinmanni* from Fulford Cave, and the springtail *Onychiurus steinmanni* from Glenwood Caverns and Hubbard's Cave. A tiny new springtail species found in several Colorado caves was named *Onychiurus nathanieli* after David and Debbie's son Nathaniel by Dr. Jacek Pomorski, a biologist and taxonomist in Poland.

Cave invertebrates are being studied to find new and rare species, provide insight into cave life evolution and biodiversity, to help protect cave life, and to learn what lives beneath the earth in the numerous caves of the Rocky Mountains.

David is the owner of Professional Wetlands Consulting, Inc. where he works as a wetlands biologist and rare plant specialist. David Steinmann is an active member of the National Speleological Society, the Colorado Grotto, the Society of Wetland Scientists and Trout Unlimited. He has also discovered several new fern species while out exploring for caves. David is often found underground in total darkness, searching for new species, with his caving headlamp providing the only light.

Back Cover: A great horned owl, a predatory bird that likes to nest in the entry areas of caves and on the rocky limestone cliffs that are often associated with caves. Great horned owls can sometimes be seen in the early morning and late evening. They are nearly silent in flight, allowing them to surprise prey such as mice, voles and rabbits.

www.ingramcontent.com/pod-product-compliance
Lightning Source LLC
Chambersburg PA
CBHW041534280526
45792CB00004B/1495